D1273625

In the Footsteps of Explorers

Peary & Henson

The Race to the North Pole

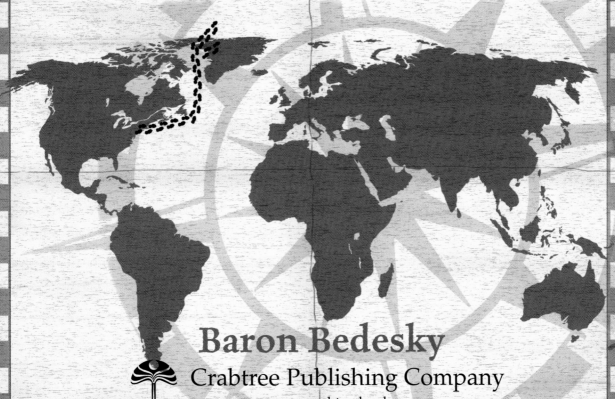

Baron Bedesky

Crabtree Publishing Company

www.crabtreebooks.com

Crabtree Publishing Company
www.crabtreebooks.com

For Jade and Katherine, fellow travelers in my personal expedition

Coordinating editor: Ellen Rodger
Series editor: Carrie Gleason
Editors: Adrianna Morganelli, Rachel Eagen
Design and production coordinator: Rosie Gowsell
Cover design and production assistance: Samara Parent
Art direction: Rob MacGregor
Scanning technician: Arlene Arch-Wilson
Photo research: Allison Napier

Consultants: Genevieve LeMoine, Curator and Registrar Peary-MacMillan Arctic Museum and Arctic Studies Center, Bowdoin College, Brunswick, Maine; Susan Kaplan, Director of the Peary-MacMillan Arctic Museum; Mildred Jones, Peary-MacMillan Arctic Museum

Photo Credits: Library of Congress, Washington D.C., USA,/Bridgeman Art Library: p. 23 (bottom); Private Collection, Boltin Picture Library/Bridgeman Art Library: p. 23 (middle, top right), p. 24; Private Collection, The Stapleton Collection/Bridgeman Art Library: p. 15 (bottom), p. 19, p. 22; Royal Geographical Society, London, UK,/ Bridgeman Art Library: p. 20; Corbis: p. 11; Bettmann/Corbis: cover, p. 5 (bottom), p. 9 (bottom), p. 27 (bottom), p. 29 (bottom); Latreille Francis/Corbis/ Sygma: p. 31(bottom left); Hulton-Deutsch Collection/Corbis: p. 8 (top); Karen Kasmauski/Corbis: p. 25 (bottom);

Michael Maslan Historic Photographs/Corbis: p. 24 (bottom); Stapleton Collection/Corbis: p. 7 (bottom); Underwood & Underwood/Corbis: p. 28; The Danish Arctic Institute: p. 25 (top); Getty Images/Getty Images: p. 17 (bottom); Hulton Archive/Getty Images: p. 26 (bottom); Photo by George Skadding/Time Life Pictures/Getty Images: p. 29 (top); The Granger Collection: p. 9 (top), p. 10, p. 17 (top); Mary Evans Picture Library/ The Image Works: p. 13 (bottom); Topham /The Image Works: p. 18, p. 26 (top); North Wind Picture Archives: p. 8 (bottom), p. 12, p. 14 (middle); Other images from stock photo cd

Illustrations: Dennis Gregory Teakle: p. 4

Cartography: Jim Chernishenko: title page, p. 6

Cover: American explorers Robert E. Peary and Matthew Henson explored the Arctic together on seven expeditions. On their final expedition in 1908-1909, they reached the North Pole.

Title page: The geographic North Pole is located at 90 degrees latitude.

Sidebar icon: Polar bears live in the icy Arctic areas of Canada, Greenland, Alaska, Russia, and Norway.

Crabtree Publishing Company
www.crabtreebooks.com   1-800-387-7650

Cataloging-in-Publication Data
Bedesky, Baron.
Peary and Henson : the race to the North Pole / written by Baron Bedesky.
  p. cm. -- (In the footsteps of explorers)
Includes index.
ISBN-13: 978-0-7787-2426-1 (rlb)
ISBN-10: 0-7787-2426-3 (rlb)
ISBN-13: 978-0-7787-2462-9 (pbk)
ISBN-10: 0-7787-2462-X (pbk)
1. Peary, Robert E. (Robert Edwin), 1856-1920--Juvenile literature. 2. Henson, Matthew Alexander, 1866-1955--Juvenile literature. 3. Explorers--United States--Biography--Juvenile literature. 4. African-American explorers--United States--Biography--Juvenile literature. 5. North Pole--Discovery and exploration--Juvenile literature. I. Title. II. Series.
G634.B43 2006
910.9163'2--dc22

                                                    2005035776
                                                    LC

**Published in
the United States**
PMB 16A
350 Fifth Ave.
Suite 3308
New York, NY
10118

**Published
in Canada**
616 Welland Ave.
St. Catharines
Ontario, Canada
L2M 5V6

**Published in the
United Kingdom**
White Cross Mills
High Town, Lancaster
LA1 4XS
United Kingdom

**Published
in Australia**
386 Mt. Alexander Rd.
Ascot Vale (Melbourne)
VIC 3032

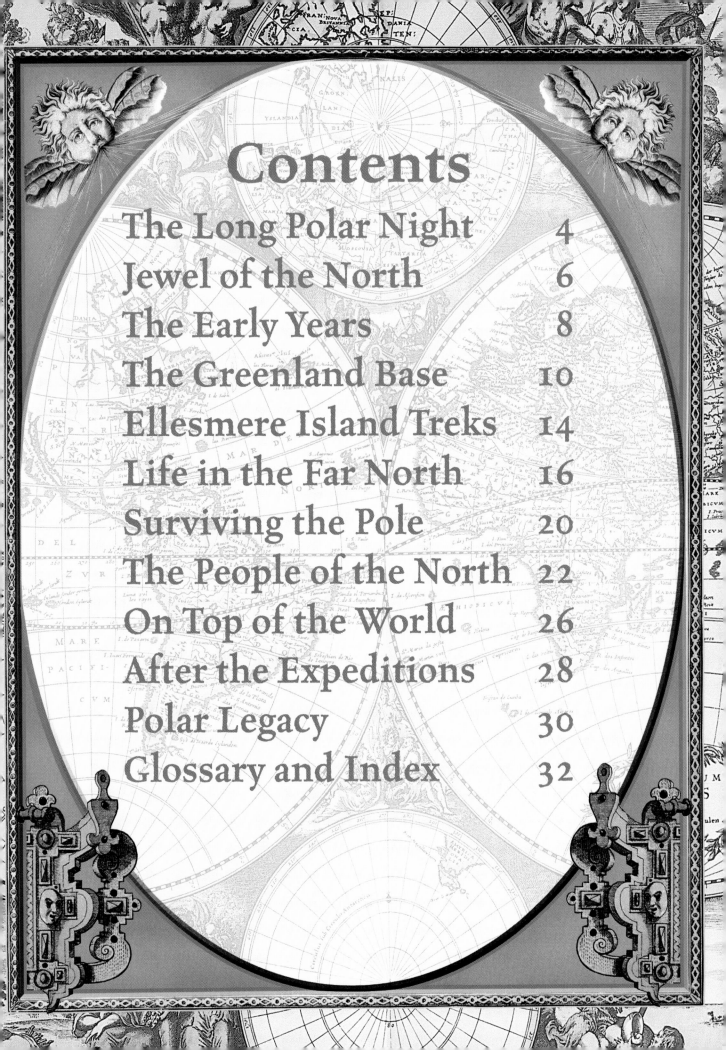

Contents

The Long Polar Night

Robert Peary and Matthew Henson were American explorers who gained fame for their repeated quests to reach the North Pole. They are credited as being the first men to make it to the pole and were considered heroes of their time.

Years of Work

Peary and Henson made seven **expeditions** to the Arctic together beginning in 1891. Until the last, each expedition fell short of the true goal — the North Pole. In 1908, after Peary toured the United States to raise funds for another trip, the pair began their last **assault** on the pole. Peary and Henson finally reached their goal in 1909 along with their **Inuit** guides Eginwah, Seegloo, Ootah, and Ooqueah.

Henson (right) was first hired by Peary (above) as his valet, or personal servant. Henson reached the North Pole about 45 minutes before Peary did. Henson's accomplishment was often dismissed because he was an African American competing in a field dominated by white Americans and Europeans.

Getting Credit

Over time, experts agreed that Henson deserved credit for his role in reaching the North Pole with Peary. Henson, like Peary, is now widely **acclaimed** as a great explorer. The work of the Inuit, or Inughuit, guides from northwest Greenland has only recently been recognized. Henson's biography describes his feelings upon reaching the pole.

"...The hoisting of the flag was not the occasion of any riotous outburst of feeling. The Commander (Peary) merely said in English, 'We will plant the Stars and Stripes at the North Pole,' - and the Stars and Stripes were planted. Speaking in the Eskimo language, I then proposed three cheers, which were heartily given... As I stood there at the top of the world and thought of the hundreds of men who had lost their lives in the effort to reach it, I felt profoundly grateful that I, as the personal attendant of the Commander, had the honor of representing my race in the historic achievement."

(below) The expedition plants a flag on the top of the world.

- May 6, 1856 -
Robert Peary is born in Cresson, Pennsylvania.

- August 8, 1866 -
Matthew Henson is born in Charles County, Maryland.

- 1877 -
Henson finds a job on a ship as a cabin boy.

- 1886 -
Peary makes his first Arctic expedition and explores Greenland.

Jewel of the North

In the late 1800s, expeditions from Great Britain, Europe, and the United States set out to conquer the North Pole. The pole was one of the world's last unexplored territories and a challenge for explorers.

Heroes of the Day

During the 1800s and 1900s, explorers often competed against each other for the glory of finding new lands. They were seen as heroes who lived dangerous and exciting lives. The public read about their adventures and discoveries in newspapers, magazines, and books.

Fame and Fortune

Many explorers were aware of the fame and riches they could receive after a successful journey. Businesses and other organizations sometimes paid them money in exchange for speeches. Their explorations were supported because the discoveries brought honor to the organization or the explorer's country. Expeditions also created opportunities for trade.

(background) The North Pole was an idea as much as a real place. The actual pole is a mass of ice covering the Arctic Ocean.

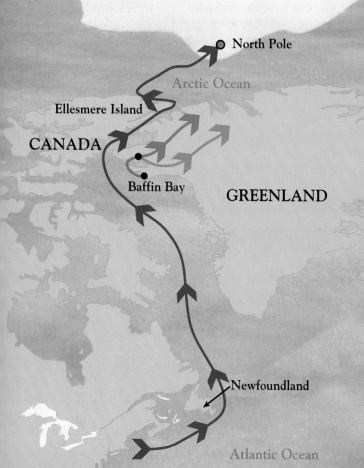

North Pole

Arctic Ocean

Ellesmere Island

CANADA

Baffin Bay

GREENLAND

Newfoundland

Atlantic Ocean

Greenland routes 1892: →→→

1893-1895: →→→

Peary & Henson's route to the North Pole 1909: →→→

The Quest Continued

Teams of explorers from Norway, Italy, England, and the United States all attempted to reach the North Pole. Slowly but surely, each group made it further north but they often met with disaster and many people died on the quest. Those who survived later published their stories.

The Northwest Passage

The earliest Arctic explorers were not searching for the North Pole. Their goal was to find a Northwest Passage, or an Arctic water route from Europe to Asia. The crews of many ships that searched for the passage met their deaths in the Arctic. English explorer John Franklin led a two-ship Northwest Passage expedition in 1845. Franklin, the ships, and 100 men became stranded in ice for three winters. Low on food and without hope of rescue, the crew starved and froze to death.

John Franklin's crew set up camp on the cold shores of the Arctic Ocean. Failed expeditions such as Franklin's taught future polar explorers lessons in Arctic survival.

- 1616 -

William Baffin and Robert Bylot search for the Northwest Passage.

- 1818 -

John Ross makes contact with polar Inuit while searching for the Northwest Passage.

- 1850 -

The first of many searches for John Franklin, lost in the Arctic. It took many years for people in England to learn of Franklin's fate.

The Early Years

Robert Peary and Matthew Henson came from very different backgrounds. Peary was a white man who attended college and served in the United States Navy. Henson was the son of black sharecroppers who was orphaned at a young age and received little formal education.

Joining the Navy

Robert Peary's father died when he was a child. He grew up with his mother and later attended college. After school, he moved to Washington, D.C., and got a job with the United States Navy's Corps of Engineers.

(above) Peary wore the warm fur garb of the Inuit when exploring in the Arctic.

(below) Robert Peary graduated with a degree in civil engineering from Bowdoin College in Brunswick, Maine. His scientific education and surveying skills helped him in his later expeditions in the Arctic.

Nicaragua

By 1884, Peary was sent by the U.S. Navy to Nicaragua, a country in Central America. He was to **survey** the area and find a possible location for a canal to connect the Atlantic and Pacific oceans. Peary became interested in the Arctic after reading the stories of those who had explored the area. He decided that he would also become an Arctic explorer.

First Arctic Journey

In 1886, Peary visited Greenland and attempted to cross its **ice cap** by sled. He traveled 100 miles (161 kilometers) inland before severe weather forced him to turn back. Peary's journey over the ice-covered land helped him determine that Greenland was an island, something not known at the time. Peary returned home but vowed to make another trip.

Henson sits near the sledges used to carry the expedition to the North Pole in 1909. The curved runners made the sledges easy to turn.

Cabin Boy

At the age of 12, Matthew Henson left his home in Washington, D.C. He went to nearby Baltimore, Maryland, and got a job on a ship where he first served as a cabin boy and later as an able-bodied seaman. The ship's captain took responsibility for Henson and trained him. He also encouraged Henson to learn foreign languages on his travels.

Traveling the World

As a sailor, Henson traveled all over the world. He left the ship at 18 and worked a series of jobs before moving back to Washington to work for a haberdasher, or a supplier of men's furnishings and clothing. In Washington in 1886, Peary visited the haberdasher to buy a hat and met Henson there. This chance meeting led to Peary hiring Henson as his valet on his next naval assignment. As Henson's skills grew apparent to Peary, he became more than a valet.

Team Player

Robert Peary and Matthew Henson made eight expeditions together, seven of them to the Arctic. Many other men at the time dismissed Henson because of the color of his skin, but Peary knew Henson was the most capable member of his expedition team. Peary trusted Henson's loyalty and skills in living in the north.

Matthew Henson learned Arctic survival skills, including the importance of wearing animal skin and fur.

The Greenland Base

Greenland is a massive Arctic island located between Europe and North America. It was the base for many of Peary and Henson's polar explorations. In Greenland, they met the Inuit people who would help them survive in the harsh climate.

STARS AND STRIPES NAILED TO THE NORTH POLE

DR. FREDERICK A. COOK — APRIL 21 1908

COMMANDER ROBERT E. PEARY — APRIL 6 1909.

TWO DAUNTLESS AMERICANS WHO REACHED THE GOAL OF A THOUSAND YEARS AND PLANTED THE STARS AND STRIPES UPON THE AXIS OF THE WORLD.

Peary craved the fame and attention that a successful expedition to the North Pole eventually gave him. This postcard was printed at a time when explorer Frederick Cook was also thought to have reached the pole.

An Important Island

Peary was drawn to Greenland for two reasons. He wished to be the first person to cross the island, and he believed the northernmost part of Greenland was the best way to reach the North Pole.

(background) Peary launched trips further north from his ship or from his mainland living quarters.

Fame and Fortune

Peary wanted to become famous and he once wrote in a letter to his mother, "Remember, Mother, I must have fame." A successful exploration of Greenland would not only bring him fame, but the money to continue. He would be paid to give speeches, and wealthy people and businesses would be more likely to give him more money for future trips to the Arctic.

Building a Team

Before leaving for Greenland, Peary assembled a team of men with skills in **navigation** and exploration. Each member was an expert in his field. This team included Henson, a doctor named Frederick Cook, a **mineralogist**, hunters, skiers, and even Peary's wife Josephine.

Preparing For Winter

After arriving in Greenland near the present-day settlement of Qanaaq, expedition members built a two-room timber and canvas building that served as the group's living quarters and supply facility. It was called Red Cliff House.

(below) Josephine Peary was a strong woman who also had a taste for adventure. She accompanied her husband instead of being apart from him for months. At the time, women rarely accompanied their explorer husbands on long voyages. During the second expedition in 1893, Josephine Peary gave birth to their daughter Marie in Greenland.

- 1886 -
Peary expedition in Greenland onboard the *Kite*.

- 1893 to 1895 -
Peary's expedition maps northwest Greenland

- 1896 to 1902 -
Peary and Henson begin another quest to reach the pole.

- 1906 -
Peary expedition onboard the *Roosevelt*. The search for the pole switches to Baffin Island.

Traveling by Dog and Sledge

Peary and his team spent several months getting to know the local Inuit population. They believed they had much to learn from them if they were to make a successful run at the North Pole. They learned hunting skills and how to transport supplies using dogs and sledges. Inuit women made protective clothing for the expedition from animal fur. Over several expeditions, Peary and Henson explored and mapped much of northern Greenland.

Difficult Conditions

Many of the trips taken by the expedition were difficult and dangerous. Cold temperatures, high winds, and heavy snow made for challenging travel conditions for the men and the dogs that pulled the sledges. They carried supplies but they also stored food in **caches** along the way. Peary set up the cache system because he knew that having enough food was vital but carrying heavy loads meant travel would be slower. Even so, in 1894, the expedition could not find the caches and had to turn back. This added another year on to the trek.

Peary and Henson learned how to make sledges and handle sled dogs from the Inuit. Dogs made traveling easier and were important to the Inuit.

Food Was Scarce

Sometimes the explorers hunted and fished for food if their supplies ran out. If no food was caught, they often killed and ate the weakest dogs just to survive. In extreme cases, the men would even eat their own clothing or boots, which were made from animal skins.

The expedition learned to make Inuit snow houses, or igloos. While exploring, they slept in igloos with fur-lined floors.

Peary brought Arctic curiosities to museums in the United States, including three large iron meteorites, the bones from Inuit graves, and six living Inuit people. The Inuit had used the meteorites for centuries to make tools, such as arrowheads. Peary sold the meteorites to fund his expeditions.

Raising Money

Each attempt to reach the North Pole cost Peary thousands of dollars. To raise money to fund the expeditions, Peary gave many speeches. Peary had many wealthy friends who also provided sponsorship money. In return, he would often name various northern locations after his sponsors. Over time, these sponsors formed the Peary Arctic Club and played an important role in funding all of Peary's future expeditions.

Ellesmere Island Treks

After three trips to Greenland, Peary decided to use Ellesmere Island as a starting point. Ellesmere is a large Arctic Ocean island located west of Greenland in the northernmost part of Canada.

Fort Conger

Previous Arctic explorers had used Ellesmere Island as a base of operations. It had an outpost building constructed years earlier. The outpost was called **Fort Conger**. In July 1898, the expedition members sailed for Ellesmere onboard the ship *Windward*. Once there, the next goal was to reach Fort Conger.

Frostbite

Peary, Henson, and expedition member Dr. Tom Dedrick reached Fort Conger with dogs and sledges but not without cost to Peary. He suffered severe frostbite to his feet and Dr. Dedrick was forced to **amputate** eight toes. The group had to return to the ship.

Peary broke a leg in Greenland on an earlier expedition. Frostbite later took several toes. Nothing prevented him from reaching his goal.

(background) Inuksuits are rock markers that stand out in the Canadian Arctic. Explorers sometimes left messages on these cairns, or piles of rocks.

Open Water

The men continued to live in the Arctic but would not make another attempt to reach the pole until 1902. In March of that year, Peary and Henson began to cross the Arctic Ocean from the northernmost point of Ellesmere Island but were forced to turn back when they reached a "lead," or an area of open water that was not frozen over. By late 1902, they finally returned to the United States after a four-year absence.

The Sixth Trip

On Peary and Henson's second voyage to Ellesmere, and sixth expedition to the Arctic in July 1905, they sailed on a new ship called *Roosevelt*. Peary designed the *Roosevelt* for Arctic travel. It had powerful engines, a thick **hull**, and was made to cut through the ice.

Help From the Inuit

The expedition spent the winter on Ellesmere and with the help of the Inuit, they hunted for musk ox and caribou. In February 1906, Peary and Henson made another push toward the North Pole using dogs and sledges. Open water and severe storms **hampered** their progress. They were again forced to turn back because of the bad weather and a shrinking food supply. Their journey set a new record by traveling farther north than anyone else had ever done and the expedition returned to the United States late that year.

Peary designed the Roosevelt *to travel where no other ship had successfully traveled before. The* Roosevelt's *hull was 30 inches (66 centimeters) thick and could withstand the crushing pressure of the Arctic ice.*

Life in the Far North

Before they could explore the North and even try to reach the North Pole, Peary and Henson had to learn how to survive in such a difficult environment. They grew more knowledgeable with every expedition, and became experts at preparing for life at sea and at base camps in the Arctic.

Packed with Supplies

For every voyage to the Arctic, the ship Peary chose was packed with supplies including coal, lumber, canvas, sledges, tools, weapons, lamps, oil, and plenty of food such as canned meat, vegetables, and fruit. Once they arrived in the far north, the ship stopped to pick up sled dogs, Inuit guides, and Inuit women who sewed the explorers' clothing from animal hides.

Polar exploration was not possible without the guidance and expertise of the Inuit who lived in the far north. Peary and Henson often traded tools, weapons, and food with the Inuit in exchange for their dogs and help while on the journey.

Henson and members of the expedition sit on a sledge aboard the Roosevelt. Their clothing, made from fox and bear fur, and seal and caribou skin, was sewn by Inuit women.

Respected Men

Peary was loyal to Henson and other team members who respected his authority. Peary was an expert navigator and surveyor who cared about the safety and well-being of his team. His system of setting up caches, or stockpiles of food, and traveling in stages on the exploration route, made it possible to reach the pole. Henson learned the Inuit language and was respected by the Inuit. They taught him how to build igloos, drive a dogsled, and how to hunt. When the food began to dwindle, the men hunted and fished for musk ox, caribou, Arctic hares, seals, walrus, whales, and fish.

The Roosevelt *at anchor. The ship's captain, Robert Bartlett of Newfoundland, also explored with Peary and nearly made it to the pole.*

Navigating in the Arctic, near the North Pole was difficult. When using a magnetic compass, explorers had to compensate for the difference between the magnetic North Pole and the geographic North Pole. The geographic North Pole is the northernmost point on the Earth's surface at 90 degrees North. The magnetic North Pole is where compass needles point to, and is several degrees south and west of the geographic, or "true" North Pole.

Housing in the North

Peary and Henson learned it was best to transfer the *Roosevelt*'s supplies to a base camp once they stopped sailing because the ship could be crushed by shifting ice. A base camp was often made from wooden planks or timbers brought from the south because there were no trees in the far north. Other materials such as canvas, blankets, and even animal skins were used for **insulation**. A stove was set up inside for cooking and to provide enough warmth to keep everyone comfortable.

Location, Location, Location

Arctic explorers relied on special instruments in order to identify their exact location. Peary's early training as an engineer and surveyor was valuable in taking measurements and developing a plan to reach the pole. He also kept a journal. To be taken seriously, explorers had to have proof to back up their claims.

Peary used a telescope on the final push to the pole. Peary also used a sextant, an instrument made up of a telescope, a mirror, and a curved measuring scale. It records the angle of the Sun in the sky when compared to the horizon, where sky meets land.

The men of Peary's expeditions had to get along and listen to their leader. Their survival depended on co-operation. Team members who would not take orders from Peary were ousted.

Greenland Stew

The Inuit are hunters who ate meat such as caribou or seal, whale, and fish. Most meat was eaten raw or partially cooked. Blubber, **organ meat, and whale skin were important foods. Peary and Henson brought their own foods to Greenland and Ellesmere Island, but also ate Inuit food.**

Ingredients:
2 pounds (1 kg) meat (traditionally seal, whale, caribou or reindeer, or hare, but beef, lamb, or rabbit can be substituted)
1 onion
1 to 2 carrots
Frozen or dried herbs for seasoning
8 cups (2 liters) cold water
1/3 to 2/3 cup (100 to 200 ml) barley, oats, or rice
Salt to taste

Directions:
1. Add water, meat, vegetables, and herbs to pot and boil heavily until meat is nearly tender.
2. Add rice, barley, or oats and boil again.
3. Add salt to taste.

Surviving the Pole

From the bitter cold to the six months of darkness a year, many obstacles had to be overcome for Peary and Henson to reach their goal. They would not have made it if it were not for years of preparation and experience.

Traveling in the Arctic

Henson and Peary did most of their traveling with sledges pulled by dogs. They also used skis, snowshoes, and even walked when necessary. At the time of their expedition, there were no planes or motorized vehicles that could work in the extreme cold. A strong team of dogs not only had to be able to pull the men, but also hundreds of pounds of supplies.

Crossing Ridges

The North Pole is not located on land, but on the frozen ice of the Arctic Ocean. The ocean currents cause the ice to shift and create ridges as high as 50 feet (15 meters). These were difficult to cross with dogs and sledges loaded with supplies. The sledges were often unloaded and reloaded several times in one day while the men created a path over the ridges with ice axes.

Peary was an expert skier and snowshoer, even after the loss of several toes made it difficult to walk and keep his balance.

(background) During the summer months at the pole, the Sun shines constantly for six months in a row. It sinks lower in the sky during the evening but never drops below the horizon. Summer's constant Sun is followed by six months of darkness and twilight during winter.

Thin Ice

Thin sea ice was a worry. In the late winter, when the team made their final attempts at the pole, ocean currents sometimes broke up the ice and created huge areas of open water. The open water eventually froze again but the expedition risked breaking through into the open Arctic. The dogs and sledges were often sent over thin ice on their own and the men followed behind.

Little Sleep

Peary and Henson realized that because of all the dangers of traveling over the frozen ocean, they had to make their final dash to the pole as quickly as possible. On the final push, they frequently covered 30 to 35 miles (48 to 56 kilometers) per day and slept very little because they knew the upcoming spring thaw would break up the ice and possibly leave them stranded.

Sled dogs sleep outside in all types of weather, curling up to keep warm. Expedition members fed the dogs pounds of seal or other meat every other day. A good team of dogs could pull 40 to 70 miles (64 to 113 kilometers) in a day.

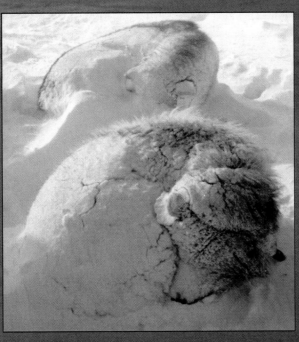

- Clothing -

Explorers learned a great deal from the Inuit people who lived in the area. For example, they learned that it was best to wear several thin layers of clothes rather than one thick layer. Many of these clothes were made from the skins of animals native to the Arctic. Men often wore the same clothes day after day. There was no running water, bathrooms, or electricity to use for washing.

The People of the North

The word Inuit means "the people" in the Inuit language. The lives of the Inuit of Canada and Greenland have changed a lot since the early days of polar exploration.

Living Off the Land

In the late 1800s and early 1900s, the Inuit were **nomadic** hunters. They lived too far north to farm and there were no stores from which to buy food. Instead, the Inuit hunted and fished for food. They used animal skins for clothing and bones to make tools such as axes and harpoons. Even needles for sewing were made from animal bones with **sinew** used as thread. Whale blubber, or fat, was eaten and used to light stone lamps. No animal part was wasted.

Traditional Inuit Clothing

When Peary and Henson visited the Arctic, the Inuit had not yet adopted European clothing. Many had never seen Europeans, Africans, or Americans. They wore two layers of clothing, including an inner layer with pants worn fur-side in, and moss-lined socks. The outer layers were worn fur-side out. The Inuit stripped half naked when they came from outside to inside. They knew it was best to remove damp sweaty clothing to keep warm.

Inuit hunters traditionally harpooned seals at breathing holes in the ice with weapons carved from bone or narwhal tusks.

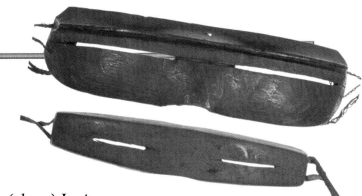

Inuit Homes

In the summer months, the Inuit lived in stone homes or tents made from seal skin. Winter homes were often made of blocks of snow. The entrance to a winter snow igloo was burrowed through the snow and was lower than the floor of the igloo to maintain warmth. Inside was a platform made of snow. Two or three large animal skins were laid on it to form a bed. Blubber lamps and the body heat of people in the igloo kept the igloo warm.

(above) Inuit snow goggles were made from wood and antler. The goggles protected from snow blindness. Snow reflects light, and in an environment surrounded by white snow, the light can be blinding. The slits in the eyepieces allowed just enough light to see.

Nomadic Lives

At the time of Peary and Henson's exploration, the Inuit moved from place to place. They hunted different animals in different seasons. Birds were hunted in spring and summer. Caribou were hunted in the fall. In northwest Greenland, the Inuit hunted walrus and whales in spring and summer. Seals were hunted all year. The Inuit governed themselves, and usually relied on a group of **elders** within their community to make decisions that affected the entire community.

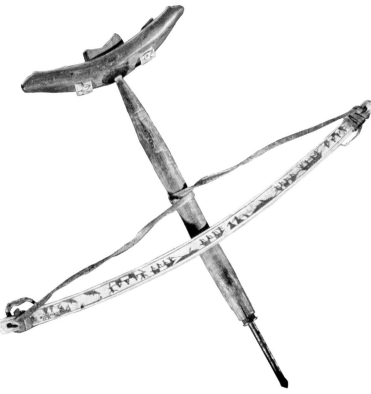

(above) Bow drills, such as this one made from walrus tusk, were used to start fires.

(left) This historic image shows a seal hunter in his kayak. The Inuit used kayaks to travel Arctic waterways during the warmer seasons.

New York in the late 1800s must have seemed frightening to a group of Inuit from Greenland.

An Inuit in New York

When Peary returned from an expedition to Greenland in 1897, he brought back six Inuit, including 14-year-old Minik Wallace and his father. He also brought back the bones of several others, which were purchased by the American Museum of Natural History in New York. Most of the Inuit died in New York, including Minik's father. Minik thought his father was buried according to Inuit custom, but instead his father's body was dissected, studied, and reassembled for display. Years later, Minik became very upset when he discovered what had happened. He demanded the return of his father's bones. Minik went back to Greenland for a while, but he never felt completely at home there or in the United States.

Trade and Religion

The Inuit began trading with European whalers who came to hunt whales in the Arctic in the 1800s. In Greenland and Canada, **Christian missionaries** from the south came to convert the Inuit, setting up near fur trading posts. By the time of Peary and Henson's expeditions in the Arctic, missionaries were quickly replacing the traditional Inuit religion with Christian beliefs. Trading for guns and ammunition also changed the way the Inuit hunted. Through religion and trade, the Inuit were encouraged to settle in one place.

Modern Inuit art, carved from soapstone that was once used to make bowls and pots, is popular among southern art collectors. The art depicts Arctic animals, myths, and stories.

Staking Claims

The Inuit way of life began to change almost immediately after contact with Europeans and North Americans. The exploration of the Arctic made the governments of Denmark, which controlled Greenland until the 1980s, and Canada want to permanently claim territory in the eastern Arctic. To do so, they set up police or army bases, or government offices in the far north. They encouraged the Inuit to settle permanently in these communities, often in **prefabricated** houses. In the 1950s in Canada, police began killing Inuit sled dogs to force the Inuit to give up their nomadic way of life. In Greenland, the government moved many Inuit from their traditional lands in the 1950s, after a U.S. air base was built.

During their lengthy stays in the Arctic, both Peary and Henson had children with Inuit women in Greenland. This was not unusual for explorers who spent so much time far from home. Peary had two sons with an Inuit woman named Aleqasina (above). Henson also had a son with an Inuit woman.

Store-bought food and processed food is sold at stores in Inuit communities throughout Greenland and northern Canada. Processed food is not as healthy as traditional Inuit foods such as whale, shown here. Some Inuit add to their diets by hunting and fishing.

On Top of the World

Peary's long-held dream of reaching the North Pole was realized on April 6, 1909. He, Henson, and four Inuit guides pushed their way to the pole.

Team Effort

By late February 1909, the first of several teams began to head for the North Pole on sledges pulled by dogs. Peary believed that dividing everyone into smaller teams gave him the best chance to reach their goal. The first teams would carry supplies, cut trails through the many ridges of ice, and set up supply stations for the later teams before heading back.

The Peary Method

Henson was among those in the early teams. Peary was in the last team. By using this method, Peary was sure that everyone remained organized and that he would also conserve the energy he needed to go all the way to the North Pole. Eventually, many of the men began to drop back as planned and the group traveling toward the North Pole became smaller.

(above) On April 6, after 20 years of frustration, Henson and Peary finally reached their destination. It took 37 days and four hours from their base camp. The expedition of 24 men and 133 dogs on 19 sledges, split into trail-breaking groups, support parties, and those who would push on to the pole.

(left) Peary's famous 1909 telegram announcing his triumph says "stars and stripes nailed to the North Pole."

Henson was actually the first to reach the pole. Peary arrived 45 minutes later, and after taking some measurements with his instruments, confirmed that they had made it. The men began their trip back to base camp and reached the *Roosevelt* on April 27. The ship did not make it back to a fishing port in Labrador, Canada, until September. At port, Peary telegraphed the news that he made it to the North Pole.

The Cook Controversy

Peary and Henson's excitement over reaching the pole was marred by news that another explorer had claimed to have reached it first. Dr. Frederick Cook, a doctor who served on Peary's second expedition, said he reached the North Pole on April 21, 1908. Many, including Peary, doubted Cook's claim. Cook's documents proving his claim were said to be full of errors. His claim was denied and Peary was declared the first.

Many people thought Dr. Cook, posing here in a studio image, lied about reaching the pole.

- July 6, 1908 -
Peary and Henson leave New York aboard the *Roosevelt.*

- September 5, 1908 -
The *Roosevelt* reaches its destination at the north end of Ellesmere Island.

- February 28, 1909 -
Teams of men start for the North Pole using sledges and dogs.

-April 6, 1909 -
Henson, Peary, and four Inuit men reach the North Pole.

After the Expeditions

After their return to the United States, Peary received much of the credit and attention for reaching the pole. Henson and the Inuit who had journeyed with him went back to their lives. Their achievements were only recognized much later.

Many Medals

To end the controversy over who reached the pole, a **U.S. congressional committee** examined the notes and scientific findings of both Peary and Cook. It found that Peary had reached the pole and awarded most of his expedition team members congressional medals. Peary also received gold medals from the **National Geographic Society**, British Royal Geographic Society, and the French Legion of Honor.

Peary had the fame he desired and a place among the famous. Here he stands in the center of a National Geographic Society photo. Other famous men of the time stand near him, including Alexander Graham Bell, who developed the telephone.

Henson's Book

After Henson returned, he began work on his own book telling the stories of his explorations. It was published in 1912. A year later, the president appointed Henson to a job as a customs clerk in New York City, and he retired in 1936.

Fame At Last

The U.S. Navy promoted Peary to the rank of Rear-Admiral and approved his retirement in 1911. Peary made money lecturing about his polar explorations. A part of northern Greenland was named after him as well as two U.S. navy ships. By the time Peary died in 1920, he was considered one of the most successful explorers in the world.

Finally Recognized

It was not until late in his life that Henson's achievements were recognized. In 1937, Henson was given honorary membership in the New York Explorer's Club. In 1938, he had a **glacier** in Greenland named after him. In 1944, he was awarded a Congressional Medal.

Both Peary and Henson are now buried in Arlington National Cemetery. Here, Henson's elderly Inuit son Ahnahkaq visits his father's grave. Neither Peary nor Henson had contact with their Inuit children after they left the Arctic. They never revisited the Arctic.

An elderly Henson shows the medal he received from the Chicago Geographic Society in 1948. He died in 1955 and was buried in New York. In 1988, he was reburied as a hero in Arlington National Cemetery.

Polar Legacy

Peary and Henson were not the first explorers to meet the Inuit and they would not be the last. Contact with southerners forever changed the Inuit way of life.

Increased Interest

While Peary was fascinated by how the Inuit lived, he was most interested in reaching the North Pole. He never fully learned the Inuit language and relied on Henson to translate. Some explorers who came in the years after Peary were geographers who were interested in studying Inuit culture. They spent time living with the Inuit, and writing down Inuit stories and history.

Many Changes

Increased contact with outsiders changed Inuit culture. Explorers unknowingly brought diseases to which the Inuit had no **immunity**. Over time, governments became involved in their lives and encouraged them to abandon their nomadic ways. The Inuit were also encouraged to accept paid labor instead of living off the land. Some lost the knowledge of their traditions as southern ways of life replaced Inuit ways of life.

Some Inuit began making soapstone and bone carvings, and prints in the mid-1900s, to sell to galleries and earn a living.

Most Inuit now live in permanent towns with access to schools, churches, and stores.

Inuit Territory

In Canada's far north, a new territory called Nunavut was created in 1999. It was formerly the eastern part of the Northwest Territories. This established a protected homeland for the Inuit, although many thousand still inhabit northern Quebec and Labrador as well as Alaska and Greenland.

The Lure of the Arctic

The North Pole continues to fascinate modern explorers. The pole has been flown over in an airship and an airplane. Explorers have reached it on foot and on skis. Some recent attempts have been made solo, or alone. Each attempt to reach the pole, like Peary's expeditions, is dangerous. One recent expedition in late winter 2004 to early spring of 2005, set out to retrace Peary's route. The Barclays Capital Ultimate North Expedition reached the pole in 36 days, breaking Peary's record by experienced dog team drivers and sledges with curved runners that can travel up and down steep mounds of snow.

(background) The Inuit are now dealing with a rapidly changing climate and global warming that some experts believe is caused by pollution from the south. The ice on the Arctic Ocean takes longer to freeze in fall and breaks up earlier in spring. This affects the polar food chain, making it difficult for animals and humans to get the food they need.

A crew of French polar explorers are flown back from the pole. Peary and Henson made the dangerous return journey to the Roosevelt over rapidly melting ice.

Glossary

acclaimed Praised publicly and enthusiastically

amputate To cut off part of a body, as in a limb or a toe

assault An attack

blubber A thick layer of fat on a whale or seal, used for food and for making oil

cache A hidden place to store goods

Christian missionaries People who believe in Jesus Christ and God and who do charitable and other work while trying to convert or persuade others to join the Christian religion

conquer To gain control over territory or people who live there

elders Older people who are often respected for their wisdom

expeditions Journeys taken with a defined purpose

Fort Conger The wooden living quarters of the Peary expedition on Ellesmere Island

glacier A mass of ice and snow that flows over a land mass. Glaciers are common in mountainous areas of the world

hampered Made difficult

hull The body of a ship

ice cap A year-round covering of ice and snow

immunity Resistance to a disease

insulation Material that keeps people warm

Inuit The Native Arctic peoples of Canada and Greenland

mineralogist A scientist who studies minerals

National Geographic Society An educational and scientific organization that started in Washington D.C. in 1888 to promote geographic research, expeditions, and knowledge

navigation The practice of charting, or making, and following a course at sea or on land

nomadic Moving from place to place with the seasons or following migrating animals

prefabricated A building manufactured, or made, in advance and then put together on a chosen site

processed food Food altered from its original state, prepared, and packaged

quest A search or expedition

sharecroppers Tenant farmers who give a share of their crop to a landowner as rent

sinew A band of tough tissue that connects a muscle with a bone

sledges Vehicles on runners drawn by dogs and used for transportation across ice or snow

survey To measure angles, elevation, direction, and distances of an area of land

U.S. congressional committee A committee of the senate and house of representatives that is formed to examine or study an issue and report its findings

Index

1 2 3 4 5 6 7 8 9 0 Printed in the U.S.A. 5 4 3 2 1 0 9 8 7 6